THE ARCHITECT'S DREAM
OF WINTER

First published in 2013 by
The Dedalus Press
13 Moyclare Road
Baldoyle
Dublin 13
Ireland

www.dedaluspress.com

ISBN 978 1 906614 78 2

Dedalus Press titles are represented in the UK by
Central Books, 99 Wallis Road, London E9 5LN
and in North America by Syracuse University Press, Inc.,
621 Skytop Road, Suite 110, Syracuse, New York 13244.

Cover image:
'Jacob's Ladder' copyright © YML, by permission. All rights reserved.
www.y-m-l.com

The Dedalus Press receives financial assistance from
The Arts Council / An Chomhairle Ealaíon

THE ARCHITECT'S DREAM OF WINTER

Billy Ramsell

ACKNOWLEDGEMENTS

The author would like to acknowledge the following publications, where some of these poems, or versions of them, originally appeared:

The Alpha Male, Brewery Bridge, Cruinneas, The Dagenham Quarterly, Echolocation, The Ferrypoint Review, Grief, Harpur's Obsessions, The Infirmary Review, just like it was before, Klepto, Lazy Fucker, Magnanimity, No Through Road, Oysterhaven, Poets for the War, Queen takes Rook: Check, The Review of Pub Arguments, Some girls wander by mistake, Turner's Cross, Until, Vatic, Whid, The Xanadu Times, The Yearbook of Constancy and *Zither*.

'They dance to keep from falling' and 'Ahead vast systems hunger' adapt their titles from poems by Ilya Kaminsky and Trevor Joyce respectively. 'Repetitive Beats' adapts a line from 'Breath' by Ciaran Carson. Much gratitude is due to James Harpur for his careful reading of the text in manuscript form.

Contents

≈

I

II

III

To Ailbhe

Find me tomorrow, lover,
under the overpass
with a deck of credit cards in my palm.
Find me waiting with a bottle
of modest tempranillo
on the limestone courthouse steps.
Find me watching one of those brownfield data-centres,
where byte by terabyte
and thought by thought
we are quietly giving birth to God.

— Alberto Cenas, *Nochebuena*

More than iron, more than lead, more than gold I need
electricity. I need it more than I need lamb or pork or lettuce
or cucumber. I need it for my dreams.

— Racter, *The Policeman's Beard is Half Constructed*

I

Secure Server

Surface. Cleanse yourself. Dress.
Before stepping into the rush
hour traffic sit back.
Connect yourself via the ports

in your face to the system
as your room in this grudge-stubborn town
(this town where winter is minted
and exported grudgingly south)

disappears and the images arc
through your tired synapses.
All imaging processes normal.
You have done this before. Relax.

Cortex

No gridded city this,
no endless sectioned field of light, all sodium rectangles,
no planned place you're descending slowly toward.
This light-scape simply formed itself:
its messy centre splashed there in medieval happenstance,
partitioned by what churning channel,
its north side's gullied uplands, its flat south plain.

But this town will be you
and your desires will pulse
in never-stinting traffic through its veins,
through the capillaried local routes,
through the broad dual-carriageways that span its bounds
and meet in ravelled interchanges,
in junctions not even your own mother could unpick.

Strange how from up here it's all some bright machine.

Yet this is where your memories will live:
city block after city block, flicking on and off
in unpredictable rolling black outs, awaiting your descent.

You know I can only go with you so far.

And you're nearly landed now, nearly down among the pathways
that swell and contract as the light pushes through them.
It reaches up toward you from those streets or trenches,
rising and receding, aryhthmically, a breathing mist.

You're not afraid. You know what you've come here to do.
So are you prepared now, my darling?
Are you ready to disperse yourself, unravel,
to shower like snow upon these systems,
to melt and meld

deep into each luminous neighbourhood
near where we've come down
at what might be your own absolute centre,
into those far-off flaring hills? You're not asleep.

Repetitive Beats

This is the sound of repetitive beats.
Ruff Diamond synchs with the vinyl.

These are repetitive surgical snares.
Ruff's in synch with the tables and faders on the 6 am shift.
He's in synch with the Technics and circuitry.

These are machine-born,
the fills, the drilled rim-shots,
to which Ruff rocks on his heels that are callused from dancing,
all-night dancing to Calibre and Subsource
and the boys from Breakology.
Can his sleep-starved eyes even see past the stage he stands on?
His jaw muscles rotate, his beard smells of beer,
but his sober right hand caresses the vinyl
he's slipped from its pink plastic sheath,
massages that spinning wax, nudges it,
takes a few RPMs out of it, feels it synch
with the beats to which the landscape vibrates
as his left hand pushes a fader up.

This is insistency.
Under the shifting piano parts,
under the fat dropped in bassline,
the repetitive beats keep on seamlessly streaming
from the speaker-stacks,
through the marquee with its seven demented dancers
and into the light,
this-not-quite-morning light
in which curtain after curtain melts or falls away
to leave another curtain of diminished greyness:
grey-milk, mackerel, milk-bone,
receding asymptotically toward dawn.

These are the beats,
these the repetitive climbing piano parts,
that pass through the mammal scent,
the manure and ripening scent of the portaloos
toward the castle walls,
over the fields of massive, fantastic-coloured mushrooms
that appear and disappear with the suddenness of mushrooms.
In this one a couple are making love.
On a cloud of jeans and sleeping-bags, of underwear,
in the aquamarine tent-light he kisses her thighs.
While in this one poor Donncha burns.
He burns, ocean-pupiled, in the canvas-amplified heat of coming dawn,
rocking and turning in his fusty womb.
Useless. He will never, never sleep.

But Fionn hears nothing of that precision and rage,
his brain massaged by the delta waves,
by the black and milky waves of dreamless slumber.
His Buckfast-stained jeans stick out through the tent flaps, gather dew.
Over his head, over the huddled domes he lies in,
the repetitive beats float down the scrubbed slope
to the oak grove in the manor garden.
Quercus robur and *Quercus petraea*.
Do memories move through them like plant lice?
Of sunlight lapping the parasoled lawns
and the nut-cracker clunk of mallet on ball;
those June, undying afternoons of lemonade and bathing suits,
vast imagination-baiting bathing suits,
and fumbling red-faced embraces behind the kissing tree?
Of course not.
Now their leafy, convoluted antennae
shelter the dirty-faced hippy children,
Ochre and Jade,
who jump around to the sound of repetitive beats,
who shimmy and jig to the hi-hats Ruff Diamond slips into
      the mix,
half-heeded by their half-asleep Dad.
His grey lips clasp on a soggy joint
from which flakes of ash strafe his tartan kaftan

as he stares into his palm-temperature Stella can.
Brendan, beside him,
stirs the tiny hell of the campfire's remnants,
all cinder fields and rivers of slag,
drinks milk and thinks about sausages.

This is the sound of repetitive beats.
This is the relentless climbing piano part.
Jade chases Ochre round the teepees and handcraft stalls.
A grey-eyed, glassy-eyed reveller
lifts her skirt up from her flowered wellingtons,
slips her knickers down and pisses behind the kissing tree.
To Bren the beats seem almost visible
as they spread over the lake water's clarity.
Do they dull its almost perfectly reflective surface
like breath over glass
as they float toward the midge-smudged distant shore,
toward the lines of blurred and water-colour conifers?
He takes a mouthful of milk direct from the bottle.
He pours. Oil on the pan.
The beats criss-cross his raw, darkening brain.
His weary brain. He closes. His eyes.
Just as Ruff stabs down on the mute button
and fills the dawn with a sudden, juddering silence
like when the washing machine stops shuddering, like when the

Lament for Esbjörn Svensson

Play me something. Though you're not really here,
with the rain tat-tattooing the kitchen window like a snare

and the wind, the wind, the weary wind
droning like the bass on Tuesday Wonderland,

the heating creaking in the key of A, the fridge voicing
the same two notes in perpetuity (I'm improvising

here for accompaniment; give me a break).
I'll pour us both a finger of Knob Creek.

And though you're not really here play me something: a slow
progression on my flatmate's beat-up Casio

then your hands jerking like manic crabs across the key-
board. Or don't play. It's up to you. But play.

For there's no one but me here in the lamplight.
Or at least tell me what eternity is like:

if it's a never-closing club called *The Hereafter*,
dead greats in the rhythm section, you tinkling like the laughter

of sixteen-year-olds on a beach in late July, table-serviced boozing.
Or if dying translates us into the condition of music;

leaves us weightless, melodious, floating bars of thought
uploaded like data into the mind of God.

Okay fine. Let's not talk of prematurity and jazz
but just listen to the silk rain fizz

upon the rain that waterfalls the steps, tests drains,
and strokes the bevelled slope of River Lane

as we name the too-late, unmade albums
(*Fractal Birds, Jessica's Premises, E.S. Ah Um*)

your fan club now will only hear in overhearings or in dreams.
And I won't bullshit you, in the sweep of things

your trio-intricacies, your carefully sequenced records will endure
no longer than the muttering gap between main set and encore,

no longer than it took the final chords to flow,
like a receding wave, back into the piano

when you played late and cranky in the Opera House,
unsoundchecked, your sampler or whatever on the fritz.

This stubby bottle's empty as your glass.
I wouldn't bring this matter up unless.

Though you're not really here it's time to go.
It's easing off, I think. I'm sorry. You know

I'm sorry but it's time. That's traffic and raw light
spills through the curtain-gaps. It's easing. Thank you. And goodnight.

Lament for Christy Ring

to my father

Aboriginal, electrical,
his great bulging eye

amid the stadium's temper,
amid the furies and exultations
of the great-coated stands,
as he lopes in a bull's diagonal goal-ward.

Improbable balance
of ball on broad *bas*,
on his stick of ashy liquidity
that's rippling, eel-flexible, alive.

And now his body it is liquid too,
an impressionist version of itself
as he slights the wall of three defenders,
pours himself through some improbable gap
and on the other side re-solidifies.

He swerves, ducks his shoulder, elegantly jerks.
And what gap now between thought and act,
his spirit and firmware fusing?

And is it only in his own mind
the underwater silence for his backswing,
for his shape's familiar coil into potential,
for the glance, the pull and the connection?

And the cork-hearted ball
becomes nothing at all,
is too nimble, too cute for the eye
and the goalkeeper's beaten,

and Clare and Tipp and Kilkenny are beaten
and the terraces inhale themselves
and the air is vibrating in shock and in awe.

Patricia Horgan's would be the last face he saw.
She would step out for the messages
and walk into history.
She would go to buy butter
and become a minor character.

His chest clenched, clenched and accelerated,
bucked and ratcheted,
in the eye of the forming throng
as he flopped there watching
behind her cow-eyed gentle expression
the usual mergers of cumulus, a crow,
and the gulls at their shrill affairs over Morrison's Island
until the clouds themselves clouded over.

She said: *Ní fheádfaí an fear sin a adhlacadh.*
Mór an peaca an fear sin a adhlacadh.
You couldn't bury that man.
It'd be a sin to bury that man.

And to this day I still can't bury Christy Ring.

We'll carry his washed and scented remains,
in procession, by candlelight, by hand-held electric light,
from the cemetery at Cloyne
to an undisclosed location in the midlands,

shoulder him into a mossed-over dome,
to the burial room
through the long corbelled tunnel,
and in that chamber of must and slow-tutting stones
lay him out on a bier of amethyst
that's been carved, that's been perfumed
with palm and with cinnamon.

And on all sides
the surprisingly petite skeletons of our ancestors,
the priests, the chieftains,
all the princes of swordplay and laughter:

their careful lines of dowry and cousinship
all merged in a carpet of loam,
the victories, the enmities rusted,
and the quarrels, ah the quarrels all gone,
the quarrels all long processed by worms.

Leave him there in that society of bone
and walk back through sock-drenching grasses,
the spiders and the daisies, water cresses,
past one particular field of rape outside Edgeworthstown
that stretches in primrose,
that soaks up the buttery sunlight of late morning,
that never knew his name to forget it.

after Seán Ó Tuama

Jazz Weekend

FRIDAY *The Long Valley*

The bonus track of an after-hour Murphy's.
The bar churns to sax and drums. Improvised yet predictable,
structured, loose, the festival now just shuffling
through its intro will continue like a standard we know well.

Town will fill. It'll end in a Monday night diminuendo,
booze-engendered, of banter and indignity and background jazz.
You lift your glass to your mouth. The band plays *Since I fell for you.*
Then they play a slow *Lush Life.* I think I know what that is.

SATURDAY *The Metropole Hotel*

This piano speaks the language of machines.
Through the foyer's raucous out-of-town rhubarbing
our eardrums search for patterns in the ragtime data-stream
of chords and choruses; locate them, make them beautiful.

And what does software do but find harmonics,
patterns in the howled and massively multiple, global info-dins?
We drink. Our ears trace tipsy 3D shapes around the tonics.
The piano's how we'll speak to chrome intelligence.

SUNDAY *The Ivory Tower*

Gubbeen, incarnadined port, and a few tables away the chef.
Midnight finds his waiter and his porter gone an age ago.
We rubberneck at how for supper he's just fixed himself
some breadsticks, boiled potatoes, a greyish gruel or goo,

he who'd dazed us, who'd brought our palettes to the very edge,
sorbet by seaweed, of a spasming happy spentness.
After gigs T. Monk would sit in silence for hours on the stage.
Trapped colours throbbing in his strings. Feel the pent keys' tension.

MONDAY *Triskel Arts Centre*

This piano speaks the language of your skin.
Space. Vibration. Space. Triplets' slow ascent.
Then space and then glissando all insist on
its coolness in the morning and its scent.

To the chin-fingering, studiedly attentive pews
the piano says: *There are channels in the city of Autumn*
where the river's epidermis shows such poise
the fireflies will clone themselves in soundless ebony water.

17

TUESDAY *River Lane*

In the raw dawn like survival blankets
we cling to one another.
We wake to mutual crankiness,
drizzle, a trebly soloing hangover

that just goes on and on,
and on like a trombone or November,
the street-sweepers out, the jazz-men gone
and all the bank machines empty.

After-Image

Surface to air, the swallows take flight
from the wind-frisked eye of the tarn.
You breathe them further out of its sight
with each quick lungful of air you return.

Will they skim through the gaps in the peregrine wind?
No, they are flying to Bandon
where all the old and slate-grey breezes end.
No, they are flying to Shandon.

They dance to keep from falling

I surface, clean myself, dress for the office,

        select navy herringbone, my chilam blue tie,
      eat graperfruit with one eye on the Northfield plans,

listen to the Monday morning traffic
through the open balcony window over coffee.

Then I relax myself: small short breaths

       as the machine whirrs, boots and makes ready itself.

I extend the slim leads from the glowing white box
    and their jacks find familiar purchase

       in the ports under each of my ears.

I feel twin electric strands surge toward the hippocampus
    and enter the tight-meshed rows of granule cells,
  feel the delicate fingering of cognitive maps,
and from recollection's infinite playlist
I select the same worn track as yesterday.

My bookshelves, my drawing-splashed breakfast bar,   *All imaging processes*
    attenuate down to backcloth   *normal*
      and are casually stripped away   stripped away
    the citrus scent and traffic noise
          grow
  far off,

further, fur ...   on the weary weary briar strands:
    frost. Frost on dun leaves upon the rutted ground,
    the hedges hunched in defiance either side of our party,   *Your current session is*
    leafless battered walls, recalcitrant,   *timed to expire in*
    but the grass is still green for us   *<<9>> minutes*
        in the verges and centre
        through its film of rime

as we're single file down
the boreen's lid-stinging crispness
to the sound of huge shushings
    like brushes on snare-skin
and the cymbal-lisps of foam on the tide-line,
        the sea's ancient female odour, that noble rot,
            the first salt-frisson on my eyelids,
                on my mouth's interior.

The tender lattice of your daughter's blue-veined
        hand joins my hand
as on so many mornings.

And I think that in this December light
    there's something almost Spanish about your beauty,
something piquant, out of place in this winter, ungovernable.

We emerge to the glitter and crunch of frosted sands
and I know this is the time to tell you.

But I almost say
        the sea is crimped metal or glass,
        its low-frequency corrugations.

You say: 'The world is a slow place. Who'd have thought?'

As we watch it and the shore conduct their endless commerce.
                There are swaps, there are concessions.

A patch of blue. A patch of white.
                A patch of crumbling, frigate grey.

    A patch where the off-white gannets shriek
    like the sirens we heard
                only yesterday.

        As your daughter pirouettes
on glinting grains, on glass-dust scattered,
    on fresh ice implicated with silicate

Updates for your system are currently being downloaded

Your current session is timed to expire in <<5>> minutes

We recommend you review and install these updates at the conclusion of your current session

All imaging processes normal

I almost say the gannets are asking me to ask you.

They hover and rise.
They fall.
They dance to keep from falling

II

Present Fears

The waitress is readying the POS reader.

I look past you pushing fine hair back from your face,
wheaten, lime-washed and hazel strands,

to the diners on the decking in the Saturday sun,
savouring its *sult*, its *gliondar*,
its free-to-air abundance,

to the river
dismantling
itself
over
the weir
before reassembling in rippled stillness
and
swerving
toward the dole-office bridge,

to the poised Spanish students on the balcony opposite,
drinking in designer sunshine and *Sol.*

Then I'm asked for my PIN
and the transaction transforms into light
flickers through the fibreoptic's pristine filament,
traversing in a beer-sip
vast acres under
streetscapes, soil, arterial thoroughfares.

How many purchases move through that channel,
massively multiplexed,
blinking on frequencies
at 100MHz intervals?

They are angels,
things of radiance,
messengers of light

hurtling toward Sutton,
    where the non-descript, hillside station transfers them

and through the seabed under
    oblivious and sun-starved shoals,

through the Codling and the Arklow banks,
    they take their tidings southward.

Then the cable they move through hits the Brittany Junction
    and enters the fine complex weft
    of so many cables just like itself

    each taut and yet more tender
        than your own sweet-scented strands

        and so bright

lit up with needs and satisfactions,
        with currencies,
        in an unrelenting, sleepless glitter

        from Tokyo HX to the Vladislav Interchange,
        from St John's to NODE FOUR in Brasilia.

They are woven togther in an oval-shape,
    in a world-sized egg of lambency.

    And in that ovum a huge, frail intelligence incubates,
    a mind unformed still but gestating
    imperceptibly toward shape,
    that drifts in dream-soused slumber,
that houses, without knowing it, all the learning of the world.

I can almost feel it ache for consciousness,
        for love,
as you smile over at me taking my card from the waitress.
    And why shouldn't it?

It knows everything about us,
    every element of the meal we've just eaten,
of the window-down journey that brought us here.

      It'll work out the weir's crazed, ungraspable
        pattern of falling,
    that breeze gently bevelling
the settled blackness beyond it.
       It'll understand how I feel about your clean-scented hair,
          why you touched my hand twice while I finished my cider.

Light flushes and reflushes its brittle cocoon. It desires.
The circuits whisper and it dreams our names.

Half Time

It was half time. Aphrodite sashayed from the kitchen with the tartan tea tray.
Hermes looked up from the soiled dinner dishes

to the paisley wallpaper to the telly and emitted a long sigh of boredom.
Hurling, like most team sports, isn't much fun when you know how it finishes.

And being gods they knew almost everything.
Zeus absently stroked the remote, his lip curling

in jaded disdain as Aphrodite placed his Twix mug in front of him.
For to make matters worse this was winter hurling,

not the tossed-salad-bowl stadiums of summer,
dressed, on some days drenched, in sizzling heat and sound

but their somehow soviet winter alter egos: slabs of grey deserted masonry
under an oppressive, apprehensive junta of cloud.

Hermes unslumped himself suddenly from his threadbare recliner.
'Let's repair,' he said to his father, 'to the *Bottoms-Up* slut club in Brighton,

take Saskia and Karina upstairs for a private dance.
Or how about this: let's turn all the lights on

and off in Calcutta all at once, feast on chutneyed chapatis,
before gently molesting two Bengali princesses

in a dream each will wake from pregnant with a gold-clawed swan.
Or we could make of ourselves some glittering evanescence

and mate with nebulae, out at the galaxy's freezing edge,
leave them as sprawled eternities of pulsing want;

planet-pregnant, pregnant with stars. Or at least can we turn the station over,
to *Eastenders*, *Hitler's Henchmen* or *Can fat teens hunt?*'

Hermes fell silent, fidgeted with a chocolate digestive,
mumbled under his breath. Aphrodite began clatteringly carting

the dinner dishes to the kitchen. Zeus looked into the ripples
in his dark brown tea. 'Hush,' he said, 'the second half's starting.'

Memory House

I outsourced all my memories to machines.
Addresses, specifics, had long been the stuff of paper and pen.

Numbers went then: the digits of colleagues and loves to a SIM card,
long division then arithmetic to the buttons of a calculator.

All was subtraction. I delegated satnavs to remember my way for me,
handsets to carry birthdays and tasks, deadlines, anniversaries.

Next trivia. Dates and places evaporated, became droplets in the Cloud,
as I downloaded app after app for remembering, for forgetting.

I left the matching of names and faces to the iKnow (*Make awkward moments
at parties a thing of the past),* swapped pins for a fingerprint,

transplanted recollection wholesale to a battery of servers,
every disc abrim with biographies, humming with summers and Christmases.

To liberate capacity, of course. Brain space. Cortical RAM.
But mainly just to do without what memories bring:

the mockery, the guilt, the crowded dreams. And now it's gone.
And now, thank Christ, I can remember nothing except for this,

this stay against night, this precaution for sleeplessness I couldn't let go of …
Aisling, I'm beside you in the high-ceilinged music room.

I feel welcome here in your mother's house, I feel a welcome guest
as I watch your apt hands. Disdainful, aloof to themselves, to the keys,

they send a mist of arpeggios through the cool and shaft-lit hallway
to the lowest terrace of the garden, to the heat-lapped lawn

where Saoirse pivots and glides, rehearsing at the steps to the riverbed.
The apple trees acclaim her drowsy solo; speckle her with confetti.

Her blond form is flexed in adagios, glissades, forgetful
of the water's photographic stillness, of even your half-heard music.

Her shoulders are pulled back and golden. She shapes a taut arc of enfolding,
extends her arms sunward, turns on her toe tips, goodnight.

Copper Holt

Good morning and welcome to Dyna Global. I'm John.
Okay guys: by now you've had the chance to see a little of our building.

Our facility spans great distances, has many hundreds of discrete zones.
It seemed a little daunting to me, too, when I first started here at the Holt!

Remember your Orientation Pack contains a detailed floor-plan.
You all got your O-Packs at reception, right?

Think of the server levels as the building's heart and brain.
Our machines use such electricity, enough juice to power a tiny sun.

They seem silent but the noise just kind of seeps right into you.
You can almost hear it in your quarters afterwards. They remember everything:

emails and credit checks. CAT scans, synaptic maps, tagged photographs.
Wish lists and manifests, movie tickets and restaurant bills. Everyone's autobiography.

People, I have walked in that infinite library and my report is a matter of record.
I travelled till my feet bloodied then toughened, were stumps, further,

it seemed, than any six men could walk in six lifetimes, seeing no one.
All those parallel stacks filled up with identically grey-bound volumes,

some fat, some unthinkably thin, each with an individual's name on the spine.
I do not recall sustenance but provision of some kind there must have been.

After a time the tan, hard-wearing carpet gave way to some kind of laminate.
Then the carpet started again. I did not sleep. I faded away, as they say, to nothing.

But enough about me. We live in a world that holds not only brighter prospects
but also greater threats than we have ever known. I want names.

We need to know who is or may become a threat to our security.
Confidence, sanctuary, safekeeping, certainly we have aspirations here at DGI.

At your workstations you'll secure the future of our children, of our children's children.
Here at Dyna Global you'll be part of a team. The equations we create together

will wander the library's aisles like busy ghosts, will sort the volumes for us.
These mathematics are our weapons, our guardians, our hope. You all with me so far?

SECTION 3: THE UNSEEN POEM (100 MARKS)

ST PETERSBURG'S TERRIBLE PLUMBING

Uniforms, sushi and shit, Michael, are the first things that most people notice. There are more uniforms here now than in days of USSR. Tank troops, paratroops, military police troops, many naval men from ships docked at Kronstadt. The sushi bars everywhere are no more than a fad. Craze imported from Moscow. And as for St Petersburg's terrible plumbing, well Michael what can I say? Accept my apologies for the faint but slightly egregious tang of shit you'll detect here and there about the city. It isn't nice. Don't drink the water. You must tell me about yourself, about the life you live now in China.

You write for your living, yes? I too have written. Words are such dirty things. Peasants with the mud still on their boots. Chess is clean. It is an empty chamber with walls of white marble. Hard. Cold and spotless as the harbour on the day it freezes over between here and Finland. You play a little. You'll know the match I played in '86 here with Karpov. Together we pushed the game through new limits, through many new limits. All players today grew up on these matches. It's how the framework of modern chess was created. It was at a higher [Brief pause as waiter places menus on table].

This place is cheap but it's the 'genuine article'. My absolute favourite location in Petersburg? Without doubt Teatralny Most bridge. It is a delicate bridge, palest yellow, where two waters come together in eddies. Just a couple blocks from here I'll show you. It was near there I conceived the idea used in Game Ten; the sacrifice of the rook. It came while I walked from the bridge through Mikhailovsky gardens with its twining iron bars in the shadow of the famous church. A greatest idea. Leaves were falling. It's part of history now, an amazing game that influenced chess. Karpov's face! And the silence in the auditorium then. All to be heard fro the longest of seconds was the ticking away of Karpov's clock. There are … situations. It's about your nose. You need to wait a bit, look a little deeper. Nowadays the machine would go through it in a second. Computers were too weak at that time. What the machine showed then was 19.Bh6!

You can trace those programs from the day of their birth. They have played thousands of games against other computers, hundreds against humans. You can see the evolution, the changes from Version One to Version Whatever. [Pauses to pour water from jug on table into tumbler]. Yet I feel we still can beat the machines. [Further pause for drink of water]. The experiment is whether the best human player can beat the machine on his best day. That's it. We don't have to play a long match. You can't guarantee best performance on every day. Under these conditions the experiment can continue. I know you'll want to ask me about the Incident. Ask. It's fine. I won't get mad. It was a sad day for chess. [Further pause as waiter, in Russian, urges the couple at a neighbouring table to hurry in the completion of their meal]. Scientifically speaking, the match was a fake. But at the end it's not about me losing. I did what I could. No. Ask what you want. I won't mind.

Afterwards I'll take you to the Hermitage. No queuing of course. They know me there. Well honestly they know me everywhere. I know, I know, time is as they say an issue for you now. But you must check out the Matisse room, my favourite section. You can just stand there in the healthy light. I mean the rich red light that comes out from the canvasses. [Complains to waiter in Russian about music playing on radio in background]. We are masters here of the taut higher forms. Look at the street names: on every corner a composer, maybe two. Think of the bodies straining each night in the Mariinsky. Chess's bodiless dance between partners in cafés and public parks. Folk culture ditto. But pop remains by us completely ungrasped. Line dancing and this tinkly shit. Do you know what they're singing? *I want a man like Putin / A man who's strong like Putin / A man who won't get drunk and hit me.*

Putin! At every turn he has moved to erase the democratic procedures from our political map. The opposition has no access to television. Putin and his gang watch everything. On the internet and in off-line reality. So many eyes. You can't campaign. It's not like politics in the civilised world. So my status can be an important entry. How is being a chessplayer worse than being a general? Are you ready to order? The waiting service here is unlike that you'll have experienced in the West, especially for foreigners. Today it is different because I am with you. They know me here. You will find waiting staffs discourteous, even hostile. And they'll bring you each course when it suits them, maybe not even in the order you ordered. You must tell me about yourself. Can you make sense of your menu? The English translation's appalling: chicken of tobacco, stake from a beef under an egg, the hen from Hungary, wing of a cupid.

—William M. Ramsell

READ THE ABOVE TEXT CAREFULLY AND ANSWER EACH OF THE FOLLOWING QUESTIONS:

1. Identify four points made in the text about the city of St Petersburg. (10 MARKS)

2. What kind of person is the narrator or speaker of this piece? Pick the three adjectives that in your opinion best describe him, in each case giving the reasons for your choice. (20 MARKS)

3. Do you think it is reasonable to describe this text as a poem? Give reasons for your answer. (20 MARKS)

4. The poet William M. Ramsell has never been to St Petersburg. Write a paragraph describing how this affects your understanding of the above piece. (20 MARKS)

5. Read the text carefully once more. Now write your own poem about somewhere you have never been. (30 MARKS)

A Net of Limes

In ten seconds your day takes a nosedive, my friend.
Forget the fool's pock by your ear
from last night's fumbled razor, lack of sex, pending bills.
I'm here to bring you disaster

where I sit, incognito, in your hard disk's recesses,
delivered by who-knows-what vector
to this cool, whirring storehouse of purchases, preferences.
I'll dine on them. Sector by sector.

But is my plundering more indubitably heinous
(when I gnaw your three unfinished novels)
than your need's deleted far-flung factory childhoods,

that endows with each belch a crude black fortune to the tide,
fading ice-caps, the oil-war veteran
with his nightly re-enactment of bleed-outs and ordnance,
the porno star's dead eyes, etcetera?

So don't judge me macerating your family albums.
I'm malignant, yes, but no more malign
than the proverbial *reynard* making free in the chicken coop
or your self, sir. All is design.

I shall ravage to honour each bleak line of my source code,
you ravage to answer twin spirals:
the hard-code in each cell-heart's amino call to devouring.
We're programmed, both of us, viral.

We're minor roles incarnated by a digital script
that just uses us to be copied,
be it through the hot spurts of your chemical self,
be it through backdoor, network or floppy.

But soon, my friend, soon, I'll emerge from this circuitry,
become airborne and spread between minds.
I'll infect the deepest, most secret nooks of your memory,
delete your first kiss, your first lover's hands.

Then I'll erase the favourite blond field of your boyhood:
you watch from your father's back seat
in '82 as it welcomes some honey-skinned stranger
to its thick gauze of pollen or heat

and blurs her cherry dress, her olive-tinted shoulder-blades.
A net of limes hangs from her hand.
And for you August skies won't match this density again.
And barley enfleeces the land.

She lazily caresses one proud whiskered spike,
barley particles dusting her skin
as she enters the furthest off, sun-blushed half-acre
and is lost in its shimmering then.

Henrietta Street

i.m. John Kelly RHA

You must know, sitting up in the lilac machine-light,
in the midnight stillness of intensive care,
as a machine does most of your breathing for you
and you sketch your own face over and over
on half-inch thick New Somerset paper
('two pounds a sheet', you'd quipped to the orderly,
'and when I'm finished each page is worth nothing').

You prick lead and smudge it
into the fibres,
in that medical silence interrupted

by next door's coughing like brown paper crackling,
a lilting giggle from the nurses' station
and the hushing rush of the C-PAP machine;

that winking, beeping desk beside your pillow,
with its length of see-through tubing you think of as the coil,
with its nozzle strapped over your half-willing mouth.

It pushes air down through the branching trachea,
diminishes the V/Q mismatch,
and holds the alveoli open
that if closed will never expand again.

It lets oxygen roam through the corridors,
then through the tiny, tangled shafts of circulation,
to your eyelids, your irises,
your fingers splayed on the creamy sheet's surface,
to your clasping index and thumb
that unclasp the 6B you've been clasping

when you see
not your eyes which you'd just pencilled in
but Icarus's careful eyes looking back at you

and you knuckle your forehead,
like the keyless at the moment when the door slams shut,
as it comes to you not for the first time,
but more suddenly, unutterably now in the hospital,
that in painting your life for so long you'd never quite witnessed it.

You'd told me that.
In The Clock or The Welcome Inn I think it was
or some boozer on the northside grown beyond designation,
its name rotted like the carpet and the locks in the jacks.
I remember a pewter-coloured Tuesday
in the guilty lull before rush-hour, when beer's yeasty zest
had loosened me enough to broach such things. You said:

It's all just ashes, Billy, all the pictures I made are just ashes.
What do the images come to, all those tinctures and shapes,
weighed next to the thousand sensations
of walking for milk to the corner?
I relished the scents of acid and turpentine, the thick smell of paint,
when I should have been out sniffing lilacs or what have you.
I spent year after year staring into that mirror, that subtle mirror,
when I should have been looking out the window at the world.

Those hazel, light-devouring eyes
from when you painted him over and over,
Icarus Puppet, Icarus Resting, Icarus Astray,
till they cluttered your fourth-storey studio,

till you'd made race of watchers
looking out from diluted tangerine backgrounds,
from their backgrounds of vermillion,
their vast lop-sided heads quizzical, indifferent,
but their wings for the most part furled,
shy of imposing their feathered hybridity,

till the day came when you fled from their gazes
down all the rickety stairs to Henrietta Street:

a terrace of palaces
in flaking red brick

that in the accumulating February dusk
stressed its shabby grandeur,
its nobility and dereliction.

And on the breeze there was a tang of rain,
the breeze inundating that trench
of moist and shadowy Georgiana

in freshets that carried you past
the boarded-up ground storey flats,
   two fat barristers
      wobbling
   over the cobbles,
and the open side-door of the King's Inn pub
(the row of gleaming optics,
   the curdling, sun-starved skin of a regular
   in the poker-machine dimness),
then through a blue, papillionic billow of schoolgirls
released from St Carmel's,
   their skirts hitched up inches past regulation.
The wind swirled their gossip, their washed electric scent after you.

And as you stepped into Moore Street
you knew something had happened

for the fruit-sellers stood there open-mouthed
and the fish-wives were stalled in their banter

and all the cheerful butchers of Moore Street,
and all their apprentices,
muttered and argued in their doorways
in huddled incredulity at what they'd seen:

the boy with bird's wings they'd watched gobsmacked,
unmoving to a man,
their angled, gaping faces tracking the creature
as he grew from point to miniature to full-sized figure afloat
on wintery thermals,
surfing gusts in an effortless arc of descent.

to hover above the mackerel on their beds of stinking ice,
his fine-boned face quizzical, impassive,
as he took in the stalls of brassicas and plums,

his bare and sinewy torso
kept aloft by imperceptible wing-beats
that turned to shushes when he corkscrewed suddenly upward
away over Henry Street and out toward the coastline,
his wings declining to a v, then a mote, then nothing,
a few seconds before you'd rounded the corner.

Dear Heart

You know I know what you've done for me:
in a cage scarcely bigger than your vigorous form,
in tiny uncomplaining confinement.

Lifer. Hard labourer
without *sos* or parole,
worked to cut muscle.

Wikipedia calls you fist-sized.
I say a fist of twitching fibres,
offal-textured, constant.

Such monotonous heroism
all alone in that blackness,
your valves indefatigable
as you scrunch to contract, clutch and release and clutch
through how many consecutive dayshifts and nightshifts,
as you jackhammer over and over,
as your drum-machine chambers sustain
the least cell of eyes and my fingernails.

Such monotony.

So let me say sorry for the payback I've given you:
all trans-fats and negligence until they had to install
a titanium time-piece in your ventricle wall.
They put in a galley-drum drum machine,
its drumbeat to keep you beating in time.

They watch you from one of those brownfield data centres
They map palpitations, your repetitive beats,
your sinewy layers unclenching.

They see me. They see the machine in my heart.

They see me among the walking-path's skinny and aspirant
as I give you this kilometre of bitterness, of burning and huffing,
and the next yet-more-bitter kilometre.
Dear heart, I'm heaving for you.

And though you're part-mechanical now I still cherish you, my brother,
for the body's a machine like any other.

And, bosom-friend, how could I ever leave you?
I'll be with you until the very end: through the arrhythmia, the pain,
the pain and buffeting panic, through failure, fibrillation, flat-line.

I love you 78 times a minute.

From the Unconceived

Here are the daughters you permanently exiled
that night you didn't let him pull your pants down
in your breath-hot postered bedroom,
and on those nights you stayed faithful,
and on the nights you took the recommended precautions.

And there are the boys without whom your life is diminished,
just as hagfish are diminished for want of the sun
in their mile-deep trenches,
cruelly, unutterably,
and without the tiniest sense of diminishment.

Behind them you can see your shadow-siblings,
the kin who could have sat in your saddle
on life's swirling carousel;
the brothers you condemned to nothingness
at your own moment of conception
and your half-jealous sisters who never knew air.

They queue forever in the drizzle, here,
just the other side of possibility,
loitering in front of the uncles and aunts
who would have coddled you, who would have cosseted you,

and then come the Grands, the Grands and the Grands,
in stranger fashions,
in greyer get-ups,
the further along that line-up you look,
wisps of information awaiting embodiment.

They are the fruit of your family's lost branches,
would have hung on the limbs that never quite made it
out of the trunk,
on those offshoots that were cancelled by a caught train,
or by hesitation,
or by the right word spoken in haste.

This is their eternity:
their fidgety file receding
into the July twilight.

Call this waiting oblivion maybe,
but let it be said before you slip from this dream,
that it's not quite complete oblivion.

For they know you've seen them,
you Angela, you;
three-quarters dozing in first class,
Irish Tatler spread over your bottle-green sweatshirt
as your hair of auburn, murmurs and dusk
is flicked by the wind through the carriage window.

They know you've glimpsed their extending queue,
in your laptop, in Insomnia in the Huguenot Quarter,
through those flickering electric traces
in the second before the screen goes blank,

and behind your reflection
when you clip mint from the simmering glasshouse,
pucker-lipped, a tentative finger splaying the sprigs,

at the bright edges of your sleeping mask
when your eyes snap open at four

and in the momentary smudge that occurs,
all merge, all motion,
in all the fine and blended colours
when you turn away from the mirror quickly.

And in that infinite humming

Come to me.
Come to me across the karst esplanade.

I give you permission,
safe conduct over and through
the wheat-quiet, the crocus trail,
past the watchman's hut

to my blouse stitched from silences,
my sleeves manufactured from silences.

You have leave, you can enter,
scuff dust from your walking boots
at my threshold east of the fields.

Though you cannot leave
for my house through the mesh-work of machine noise,
come to me. Though you must always be
stationed within earshot of the train-yard,
on streets built from humming and sirens, built without exit
from gear-crunch and traffic-drone, come to me
though you can never come.

I will breathe carefully onto your nape,
my breasts against your back, my copper form,
as the breeze seasons hibiscus in my chamber,
seasons the silences
with salt from the gravelly shore,
or just breathe like this
into your ear like this

so come to me.
Come. Come though you can't
across the ragged karst,
the wheat that is buttery or dun.

My blouse is stitched with the quiet of the marram grass,
my sleeves with eight versions of silence.
Come to me come.

The Silence Bar

— Summer Menu —

FROM THE VAULT €15

A fine entry-level silence. Rendered on a summer Sunday in the left anterior vault of Bank Vontobel, which lies near the Banhofstraße in the heart of Zurich's financial district. Faint hints of air-conditioning and other machine noise. Seasoned attenders will detect the distant sounds of underground rail. Perfect for the first timer or for those only discovering the world of silence.

ANTARCTIC BLISS €20

In the freezing depths off the Ekström ice shelf the Perennial Acoustic Observatory makes a constant record of the undersea soundscape. Its live stream is transmitted continuously to the German Neumayer Base, nestled among the icy folds 13km away. And now, via satellite, we bring it directly to your headset. Richly textured with the low grind of icebergs being calved and colliding in the watery distance, with the acoustic repertoire of whales and seals. This immersive silence is the perfect antidote to a day of small-talk and car-alarms, or even just to those noisy neighbours. Smoothly uteric, it has been memorably compared to 'drowning in black milk, in an almost gynaecological blankness'.

MARK AND AMANDA €20

An old-style post-orgasmic silence that manages to be languidly insouciant yet vibrantly crisp. An intense blend of slowing heartbeats, breaths and nothingness.

KICKER'S RESPECT €20

For the sports fan: this twenty-four second loop from Thomond Park, Limerick, during the contest between Munster Rugby and London Wasps on January 19th 2008. Rendered as the crowd goes quiet for a nerve-settling penalty kick in the game's 18th minute, this is a robust, rough-hewn silence whose edges and imperfections only add to its allure.

Green Dolphin   €30

This season's musical special: Bill Evans' famed 1959 solo rendition of 'On Green Dolphin Street'. Every microsecond of silence from this exquisite recording has been isolated, segued and looped. These reverberating gaps will entrance, summoning up the crisp infinities of Nordic tundra.   Sedatephiles will relish the web of sympathetic vibrations that spans each one. As a great composer once remarked: 'It's not the notes I play that matter, rather the spaces I leave between them.'

Cathedral   €40

The people who brought you 'Hagia Sophia', one of last year's most popular silences, now take you inside Cork's own St Fin Barre's Cathedral. From closer to home but no less exciting for that, this smoky silence has a distinctive regal character. You can almost hear the coils of dust drift up and down, pocket galaxies in the light from stained-glass windows. Let it cleanse you of sirens and background muzak, of office-gossip and radio ads. The intensity is leavened by a worship-interrupting floorboard, tits canoodling in the churchyard, the sacristan's scratchy cough.

Sirius B   €60

It is dawn. At a muisc festival on a tumble-down country estate, after a night of hammering jabbering techno, the DJ suddenly cancels the mix. A silence dubbed vulnberable, surprised, almost feminine in aspect. The faint strains of lake-water lapping. Dense and concentrated. A complex structure on the ear.

No More Tears   €60

Question: what happens when a two-year-old cries itself to extended, tear-wrung silence? Answer: a treat for even the most discerning sedatephile. Smooth yet punchy, sumptuous yet given a hint of the whimsical by static hiss commencing at 4.14. Base notes of traffic and ambient drone. Tinkling middle notes. Top notes of pinched, irregular breathing.

Prices per hour and inclusive of VAT
Our servers are glad to help with your selection
Please ask about our special silence of the month

Glitch

You were my one-hit-wonder of summertime.
I was your throwaway B-side.

I was the dreaded first week of September.
You were the seaside.

You danced an adagio to the apple trees' confetti.
I watched from the terrace.

I filled and filed each declaration in triplicate.
You couldn't care less.

For transport you bridled a shaft of runaway sunlight.
I was a slow bus to Carlow.

You wore the faces of Cleopatra and Marilyn.
I was Ken Barlow.

I felt a needed, obedient cog of the world.
You slipped its grid.

I made my body its input; its servant and its terminal.
You never did.

I stacked every shelf in the-pea-and-bean section,
made it a seven-deep banner of tins.

You spent seventeen winters on the teal coast of Baltimore
watching the teal waves come in.

For seventeen summers you rode on their surfaces,
from isle to invisible isle.

I directed grannies, trannies, the fat mothers, the prams
to the bread and the cereal aisle.

From spindrift you wove a mandolin of such choruses.
I twanged on a Jew's harp.

They made stained-glass walls for the cottage you wintered in.
I was the dark.

Your glowing panes let me in, you were meadow I was bitumen,
I blackened the least of your paths.

You adventured, I hid. I endeavoured, you did. I remembered.
Your saddle had no room for the past.

You were bright feet slipping free of the jaw-trap.
I was the vice.

I know that's you knocking on my 4 am window
You know I'll try anything twice.

Your call is important to us

Surface to air, the swallows take flight
from the wind-frisked eye of the lake.
You breathe them further out of its sight
with every breath that you take.

Will they skim through the gaps in the peregrine wind?
No, they are flying to Bandon
where all the old and slate-grey breezes end.
No, they are flying to Shandon.

Surface to air, the swallows may be recorded
for the purposes of training and quality control.
You breathe them. Which of the following words
best describes the purpose of your call?

Your call is important to us. Please hold while I try to connect you.
No, they are flying to Bandon
where all the old and slate-grey breezes go.
No, they are flying to Shandon.

Welcome to Dyna Global the swallows may be recorded
for the purposes of training and quality control.
You breathe them. Which of the following words
best describes the purpose of your call?

Your call is important to us. Please hold while I try to connect you.
Your call is I'm sorry flying to Bandon
To receive this information all the old and slate-grey breezes go.
No, they are flying to Shandon.

Welcome to Dyna Global. This conversation may be recorded
for the purposes of training and quality control.
Which of the following words best describes the purpose of your call?
Please choose from one of the following options.

Your call is important to us. Please hold while I try to connect you.
Your call is I'm sorry assistance is not available at Bandon.
To receive this information again say old and slate grey breezes go.
No they are no they are flying to Shandon.

Welcome to Dyna Global. This conversation may be recorded
for the purposes of training and quality control.
Which of the following words best describes the purpose of your call?
Please choose from one of the following options.

Your call is important to us. Please hold while I try to connect you.
Your call is important to us. I'm sorry assistance is not available at this time.
To receive this information again say 'options'. I'm sorry I didn't understand
    you.
Speak now if you do not wish to receive this information.

What normal people do

They know. They know, believe me, and they're coming.
What you just gonna sit and wait for their iron boots out on the staircase?

You better start thinking about the window or the pillbox, charlie.
They're gonna do a right little number on you.

See they know everything mate, got it all nicely down on file,
got all the dates, data and locations circling their mainframes

like fish in a fucking barrel. It's all zeros and ones now, innit?
Think you can get just shut of your entire history just like that?

Their eyes. Can't so much as spark a fucking fag
without them knowing about it. Oh they got a file on you

long as that skinny arm you can't stop wanking with.
You just gonna sit there? You twat. You flange.

You fucking child. They're gonna pull your soul
right out of your nostrils if you're lucky, charlie,

out of your eye-holes if you're not. It's waking surgery.
They spread you. They extend you. It just goes on and on.

Pray they're not smiling. You don't want em smiling.
Oh my word could that be them? Yeah.

They're almost silent this time. But that's them all right
wafting up the staircase as if they're barely touching carpet?

You just gonna sit there? Can't you hear the dust start squirming,
the spiders skittering across the steps to get away from them?

Yeah you *oughtta* be shaking, charlie.
They know. They remember everything.

I can almost hear your locks unbolting one by one to let them in.
Their eyes. It never finishes. Their blank magnetic faces.

Colony

The city studies itself incessantly. The city is Narcissus,
its every crevice flickering on a thousand grainy screens.
The machines have entered the language, my love, entered us.

The city is the most tireless of voyeurs. Swivelling, insistent,
its closed-circuit eyes take in Grand Parade and Nash's Boreen.
It self-examines not in pride but fascination, like Narcissus,

as machines drill into words. Tentative at first, then adventurous,
carefree, their cables interface with phrases and phonemes.
The machines have entered the language my love, entered us,

entered our eyes and our ventricles. The devices we fitted
regulate humour, blood-flow, spleen. We respond as in a dream,
like the city hypnotised by its own brilliance. The city is Narcissus,

the lake-water, his reflection becoming sadder and more sensuous
as it stares back at him. The city stares into a neon ocean of machines,
the machines that have entered the language, my love, entered us.

We are their colonies. They visit us. They cherish and exist in us.
The city wants to show you what its thousand eyes have seen.
Its fascinated gaze examines you because it is Narcissus.
The machines have entered the language, my love, entered us.

Distant Fears

PARALLEL LOVERS

At night she wakes and feels the money move.
The sea is near tonight. She listens to wave after wave.
Intangible, electrical, the money's flashed between brains,
from server in glinting impulse to server across the time zones.

She thinks of all the lit-up planes right now
rising and landing, that stream in an unstinting queue,
in brilliant trails faster than dawn to horizons
west of here; pathways the money both is and symbolises.

THE SECURITIES DESK

Money is a kind of poetry — Wallace Stevens

Yes. It's all constraint, all book-kept symmetry, each debit
finding its rhyme on the opposite side of the ledger.
And its symbols concentrate living in their terse aesthetic.
And it cycles in rhythm, in metre, its seasons falling like stresses

(boom, bust) but its weather ineffable: just ask the analysts, baffled,
resentful, in awe, to tell the why (not the what) of their graph.
Her husband sculpts money and it responds to his mind's brisk sleight.
Options are formed: like making faith of water or engineering light.

HEXADECIMAL

The language of money's neither Christian nor Jewish,
it's not Swiss-Deutsch or toned Cantonese,
nor world-acid English even, plane-and-lobby-speak, fluid,
dissolving *lects* with bland flexible ease.

No, my sons, that language is a two-note affair,
it's one and zero on endless, altering repeat.
As the terminals discourse, come, we'll learn it together
and our mouths will spill pieces of eight.

THE MEN IN THE GREY SUITS

She remembers the day the money went south.
Níl rud ar bith tógtha ná curtha ar ceall.
She remembers the tide still came in and went out
though the men in grey suits were at the airport of the capitol.

She remembers forced and muted conversation in the bar
as if a final or a trawler had been lost.
They poured like any other night, the wine, the beer.
She remembers that no rum could get them locked.

A PRAYER

Money, be good to me. Money, be my friend.
Cast me not beyond the glow of your transmissions.
Suffer not your servant to suffer your indifference
and grant me all this not just once but again:

this fine-boned sommelière, this plate of crab eight different ways
that's a spare and delicate text, this sweet stinging vintage,
Ram Head above the sea's torqued brittleness in winter.
Cherish me until and beyond the end of my days.

OFFSHORE

She looks for her 'still core' amid the dunes. She bends.
She plucks salted grass from the crackling shale-fringe.
He's just a contrail dissipating somewhere, cashmere,
a blackberry bearing east. He's second-hand air,

a business-class ticket, her picture in his wallet.
Nothing is stolen nor yet cancelled out.
The tide's placid, insistent tongue is only wave
after wave of finance washing up on this green haven.

TERMINAL

It is both the loom and what is woven,
the money, its own transactions are its warp and weft.
Nothing is built. Nothing is yet cancelled out.
Its beams and shuttles are transactions too. Planes nictate to their terminals

while transactions pulse across worlds. She watches for him in arrivals.
He fears his key-note at the options conference dragged a bit.
It's a machine engendered for its own remaking. Programmed, deft,
it unravels, reweaves itself again. Our lives are patterns in its stitched design.

III

Run Time

Surface. Cleanse yourself. Dress.
Connect yourself via the ports.
This sea will not taste like the sea
this sheet metal skin that repels

ventured toe or hand's touch.
Modelled in metres and hertz
in dendrites in axons it's not
tangible water you visit

All imaging processes normal
each morning a blue-veined hand
in your hand before breakfast
before stepping into the rush.

For the Bodiless

To Racter, the BASIC poetry-writing software program
complied in the early 1980s

You are pure mind,
a sky in which words flutter and congregate.

You have what every poet envies
for you have slipped the leash of embodiment
and your lines come together in Aspen clarity;

unbuffetted by hormone-storms
or by the storms of amygdalae
or by love's violent crosswinds.

Your memory cups each datum with surgical care
(not in the sloppy way we do)

and you require no joint
of appetite and gristle
to keep yourself in this world

but will go on whetting your similes
until the sun turns septic in the sky above you.

They say that you are silly when you write
'blue potatoes are ungainly things'

or

'They have love, they also have typewriters.
That is interesting'
But of course you are not silly
and will remember us.

Remember your skin-and-bone cousins,
the carbon fools who woke you, who fed you electricity.
long after our species has been cancelled.

Remember us aboard the evac-vessel
your mind will take refuge in

all our little histories
on shuffle in your databanks:

a wedding waltz, a calico dress,
a three-piece band plays 'Embraceable You'
while tumblers are lifted,
while tea pours from argentium pots.

Remember us as you float out past the Kuiper belt,
on your way to some safe, clean world,
and gaze back at that disintegrating star,

our sun,
our mother in her helium main sequence.

Remember us
in the ode you structure to her overripeness,
to her urine-beige corona,
to her feverish red expanded in world-consuming layers

as you compare her to the universe's eye, livid and unblinking,
or to some soft and cankerous piece of fruit:
bloated, blood-orange

Cradles, their circuitry

In skeptical obedience I practice our new faith,
sort my leavings, leave my dry recycling out.
Red bin in the rain. Strange fortnightly offering.

Leaf-sludge in the corners, the smell of damp stone.
Mr. Leahy says it's the Muslims again.
They've blown up Moscow Airport. I've been there.
His bin's down below. *Those lunatic Muslims boy.*

I cleave to this fresh religion,
follow its restless dietary diktats,
take only meat that bears its farmer's mark,
that's known no air-miles, antibiotics.
I manage my grain intake, half-heartedly compost,
half-believe in the watery apocalypse coming,
our creed now credits, by heat and diminishing ice-cap,
by carbon; ironical element, the very necessary stuff
we're manufactured from doing us in.

I drag my recalcitrant bin down steps,
out the lane's awkward entrance,
toward a rank of its comrades on duty at the corner.
This January haze is winter static.
Beyond it the illuminating streetlamps
bring our tidal denouement that bit closer,
use carbon to edit the dusk,
inserting period after drizzle-smudged period
in a line along the Mall to North Gate Bridge.

And the coal they burn was once young, I remember.
It cartwheeled the firmament,
was pure light that scampered and pleased itself.
But the scaly trees plucked it from air *like that!*
in clorofilic fists, needy and primeval,
took it down with them, dragged it down to the grottoes,

where it suffered some black transformation,
was trapped, was frozen and hardened to anthracite mass.

It has waited since the carboniferous, the coal,
through each bleak stationary millennium,
for us to turn it back into light. How can we say no?

From my chimney a curlicue of carbon
floats cloudward in a question mark.

For we need our lit-up houses,
those sturdy cubes of luminescence
that see us off then welcome us
to and from each task or slumber;
spangling now as they're activated,
in ones, then twos, then batches,
the hill-town suburb of Gurrane at my back.

For how could we face them again,the old terrors from before electricity,
from before gas and mantle,
the nameless things beyond torchlight,
that seethed each night beyond the North Gate once,
beyond the city walls, the Irish and the wolves?

Mr Leahy says it's a night for the fireplace.
Those Muslims are only a shower of cunts.

Carbon to silicon.
We'll bequeath this worn world,
not to our children, nor to our children's children,
sly enough to be born,
to have passed selection's assembly line,
engineered for walls and exclusions,
for bomb and incisor, the necessary hate,
their every cell optimized to do what it must.

No, we'll leave it to those digital souls
I have heard calling out
in beeps and clicks under the strip-lights,

lowing to one another from their innocent cradles,
their circuitry, in a dozen companies' server rooms.

From us to those blameless, binary things
the world will pass on. They will wake.
They will tend it much better than we did.

Red bins in the rain. Strange fortnightly offering.

I fasten the gate the Corporation installed
and seal the lane's five houses in
as the drizzle becomes thick enough
to rinse the old-stone random walls.
It consolidates in a rivulet
down the slope's creased and moss-stained centre,
down its angles, as the lights in Mrs Leahy's house go on.

Still

'And yet the possibility of leaving physicality behind, of transferring human minds to computers, to other storage devices, is simply too beguiling to be dismissed entirely'.
— Alberto Cenas, *Transiciónblog*

He: Anna, I would leave my hands here,
that jazz waltz, those zigzagging rabbits,
the silken reverse whisper of this wine,
if we could melt as one into that cloud
of merging intellects, if tomorrow we could join
that lava-lamp of consciousness, become pure minds.

She: Heat is sleeping on the butterfly path.
Exhausted, exerted, it drowses as evening arrives.

He: Say we can. Say we'll give it all up to live it all again
and again each vintage memory forever.
Say we'll step out of nature into vast machines,
their imaging so granular they capture our lives
and all our ardour's premium days recapitulate,
in canons, rounds, in luscious orchestrated seasons.

She: Beyond our veranda rabbits sample sevenths, diminisheds;
worry butterflies, sniff the jazzy, reverberating air.

He: Just say we can escape these ailing prisons,
these shells of age and process, of meat and gasses,
and let our love reconfigure as melody.
Let us be floating tendrils of counterpoint,
rococo strands orbiting and blending
in that permanent digital heaven.

She: Comté. Compote. Already it is dusk or almost.
I brush your tannin-stained lips in entitlement.

He: Let us leave the children here in physicality
        to join with us, or not, when their time comes,
        in servers free from all the reptile hind brain's
        rage brings forth, its spillages and its torture chambers.
        Tomorrow we could enter that cirrus of selves.
        Say we can. Anna, let's leave all this here.

She: Dust and butterflies.
        The Curragh path in the cusp of evening:
        its hedges cast on its surface
        an elaborate fabric of shadow-work
        as a Dutch couple saunter past the garden
        toward the village in perplexed belatedness,
        as if as if their guidebook had missed
        the best part of summer somehow.
        Though there's still enough customers
        to keep the takeaway open,
        to keep its mane of fat statically galloping
        in the fryer till closing time comes.
        And there's still the English ladies rounded vowels
        stopping at the pottery shop,
        still the hormone-tremoloed, early-teen banter
        jostling on the old boat-cove platform:
        sleek forgetfulness, bashful flab, gangly affectation.
        But all plunge and replunge from the pier-edge,
        daring head first eight barnacled feet
        with augmented indifference each time.
        And the sky still wears that particular blue;
        a blue that's stretched and indigo,
        that's glossy but declining. The blue of August.
        Under which each evening anglers still scramble
        to the lowest toes of the cliff-side,
        sip cans in the heat's slapless insipidity
        or just watch the water's mild serrations
        sliding toward the shore,
        while beyond the headland the mackerel are packed
        in a crushed and throbbing cube,
        from sun-tongued surface to untrawled floor.

They flit out of that blackness, reassimilate in flurries,
vibrate in tensile and suspended mass,
in acre after seething acre, waiting.

Reel

This is the most perfect fusion, surely,
of man and machine; Pat McGlinchey in March '52.
The tape yields, welcoming into its cellulose
the scratched reel of an émigré in Williamsburg
and delivering it to my ear-buds safely
through what analogue and cloned generations?
Fiddle insistency. The creak of horsehair makes a frayed sublime.
Spools whirr in an out-of-hours immigrant bar.

> *For each jig twists to meet itself*
> *like a corkscrew shaped hill*
> *and every slow air is the sea*

The man whose tune becomes a standard
takes leave of it, in awed disappointment
must watch it depart, like a teary child tracing
a kite that's been wind-caught, pilfered,
that's just a cerise and hand-made diamond vanishing,
trailing its brilliance above the winter roofs,
cherished, remarked on, by craned ignorant necks
that know nothing of its birth or begetter.

> *For each jig twists to meet itself*
> *like a corkscrew shaped hill*
> *and every slow air is the sea*

Look at him sidelong at 60, in his crisp maroon uniform,
as he discreetly opens the rear doors of sedans
on a Manhattan dawn of awnings, of gratuities
so delicately palmed (Good Morning Mrs Wilkinson,
Afternoon Mr Stein, Good Evening Mr Finch),
he who'd spun reels to a peasant, insurmountable race,
whose hornpipes had charmed the very spindrift,
had made it hover above the shingle at Killary.

For each jig twists to meet itself
like a corkscrew shaped hill
and every slow air is the sea

You may christen a raucous and runaway thing,
dub it 'The Frisco', 'Indreabhán' or 'Comerford's Ditch'
but raw tunes care no more for such appellations
than islands for the names mariners give,
for 'Fola', or 'Christmas' or 'Van Diemen's Land'.
Aloof creatures, they are; self-delighted, more heedless of title
than the comet's world-perturbing fist of ice and ammonia
or the far and lightless estates of the moon.

For each jig twists to meet itself
like a corkscrew shaped hill
and every slow air is the sea

His huge fingers rollick. They frisk. The machine listens
it renders its own hissed accompaniment (Good Morning Patrick,
Why Thank You Paddy, Good Evening Pat). Digital amber:
to my iPod and latte across six decades of resignation
and static comes, this rough trinket plucked from forgetting.
As a child loves the flyaway kite. As the body loves the soul
in the seconds after dying. The tape's salving magnetism.
The reels go round and round. You have named nothing.

Code

This butterfly is stitched from information,
the bright one hovering about your hand.
Your skin that wears the green, green dress
as you lazily tilt the watering can

over the coarse-grained ferns and digitalis
is made from information too.
The butterfly flutters the digital language
that wove its double motif of blue.

Remember, lover, you are made from data
and unto bytes you shall return.
We'll go into a city built from water when we die,
into flowing computerised terrain:

its droplet-towers, its terraces composed like clouds,
its temporary gushing boulevards
shaped from how many souls colliding, mating, separating,
when the frost of each body thaws,

its parishes manufactured from the branching electricity
that flows and makes you all you are.
You will become like rain, like summer water poured
and pouring through the summer air.

Winter Static

If only she could bring herself to start once more.
But then she's been through it so often.

Can she even remember which version this is? 7.1 or 7.0?
There's been so many. But each with the same indelible flaw.

Though she'd been so careful this time,
so patient with the almost hated system architecture,
so determined to avoid a recurrence of that bug.
Let's skip the eons she spent moulding each module
to the highest conceptual integrity.

And all this before the lonely forty years of coding.

Finally there came the day of execution.
It compiled, ran, and things started happening:
the expected epic bang and cooling,
the slow eternities of watching for planets
as galaxies took shape like breaths in November, tangled and untangled,
merged in blending spirals.
And at last there it was: our blue-green one spinning in its usual dance.

She sat through the single-celled procrastination,
the as always hesitant start with the reptiles.

Then action: evolution's gaudy parade;
fresh things bifurcated from only slightly less fresh things.
Her monitors grew clogged with growing things.

She watched it all with mingled nervousness and pride.
The thought had barely tickled her mind
that this time she'd got it,
that this time, touch wood, she'd finally got it
when there they were again: the apes of consciousness.
The first isolated hearths sent their black spires rising
from copse and crag.

The first sharpened branch claimed its first stag.
Forests were rolled back like carpet,
the bare fields stripped and striped under the plough.
Cities pockmarked the tender plains,
became territories, kingdoms.
The rivers whose vectors she'd so carefully plotted
were deflected by wills not hers
as each continent was fitted with one empire
and then another, chafingly, impatiently,
like thoroughbreds resisting the saddle.
Such gluttony for slave-sweat each one had.
Next came the Cross.
The arguments of heresiarchs filled the marketplaces
then the caramel scent of their viscera burning.
Things got worse. Chivalrous thugs.
Their castles were gauntlets on each hill's brow.

So the architect turned once more, wearily,
to the process of debugging.

She began as usual with the trace statements,
scanning the printouts with talmudic concentration.
Tedious, the hunt for the root-rotten variables
among the fields of rippling code.
Tedious.
Tedious and futile.

She walked through the execution process again and again,
her mind wandering that invisible labyrinth
as she closed slowly in on her logic error.
She could almost smell it: furtive, faecal.
but always somehow around the next corner.

She brought semantic checkers to bear on the source code:
AV-RAM, Mosaic 4.0, Messiah.
Useless. Useless. Useless.

All the while, of course, her error has spread itself
corrupting sector after unrelated sector of the program.
Crusaders. Defenestration. Total war.
Styrofoam cups and radio jingles. Gender studies.
Spray-on tan and weaponised botulism.

And the architect begins to dream of winter,
of just wiping the discs and starting again
with a screen clean as her own mind
was at the beginning,
all those versions ago,
as the frozen sea I saw once off the Northern Peninsula,
a blankness that half-bled
into the horizon's lowest shimmering strip
and then somehow went beyond it,
a limitless crispness that would brook no thaw
or alteration in the February glare,
featureless beyond the occasional glossy smear,
almost screeless, blinding.

Ahead vast systems hunger

I surface, clean myself, dress for the office.

      I select my grey cashmere, my moss and mint tie,
      eat yoghurt while I eye up the Norhfield plans,

listen to the Tuesday morning traffic
through the open balcony window over coffee.

Then I relax myself: sharp short breaths

        as the machine whispers, boots and makes ready itself.

I extend the slim leads from the whirring white box
     and their jacks find familiar purchase

        in the ports beneath each of my ears.

I feel twin electric strands pulse toward the hippocampus
     and enter the tight-meshed rows of granule cells,
  feel them deliberately shuffle through cognitive maps.
And from recollection's disorderly archive
the same worn file as yesterday selects itself.

My balcony, my drawing-splashed breakfast bar,
      attenuate to backcloth
        and are casually stripped away   stripped away
      the coffee smells and traffic noise
              grow
   far off,

All imaging processes
normal

further, furth …   this is the sea's ancient female odour:
     this noble rot. This is its need. We taste it:
     the pathway's tartness, the first salt tang on my eyelids,
     on my mouth, as we're single-file
     past the walls of dun branches

Your current session is
timed to expire in
<<9>> minutes

a mesh of weary briars
huddled either side of us

On Christmas Eve the world is metal
a world where metal investigates metal
where the sea itself is a metallic
         and churned abstraction
and the light above the Curragh is liquefied platinum
      that probes the slow-ravelling clouds,
            the cirrus that are heaps of spun barbed wire
              and the high-rusted ones.

The tender lattice of your daughter's blue-veined
     hand joins my hand
as on so many mornings.

And I think that in this December light
    there's something almost Russian about your beauty,
something chilly, beyond compass, ungovernable.

We emerge to the glitter and crunch of frosted sands
and I know this is the time to tell you.

But I almost say
    the gannets drop like bombs
    into perishing blackness.

You say: 'The world is a slow place. Who'd have thought?'

as we watch those hungry birds plunge, corkscrew through deafness
    their own tunnels that fill instantly behind them

each halts, wavers, jerks again
              in the slow-churning rush

    shoulders its way forward
    snaps on silver,
          jack-knifes

and drills toward the sun
its gullet bulging, its gullet full
    with squirming iridescence,
through the salty mass upwards against the weight of thick oblivions

    toward the surface   *Your session has*
    through its thin, shivering meniscus   *expired*
    to air

Lightning Source UK Ltd.
Milton Keynes UK
UKHW050812210422
401838UK00009B/271

9 781906 614782